Dare to Believe

Looking with Intention into the mirror of God's Word

A 5 week study through the Book of James

BY MARJIE SCHAEFER

www.flourishthroughtheword.com

ISBN: 978-0-9972333-7-7

Dedication

I lovingly dedicate this book to my dear friends
Cheryl Manning and **Melody Van Peursem**.

These two Godly women embody and reflect the five themes of James: they are patient, they practice the truth, they have power over their tongues, they are peacemakers and prayer warriors. I am so very grateful for their friendship and presence in my life.
I learn from them every time I'm around them.

Appreciation

These wonderful friends have helped to make this Bible study book possible:

Kristi Knowles - edited and compiled all the information, ensuring it made it to the printer on time.

Kim Kauffman - brought her creativity to bear in the process of designing and producing our photography.

Lisa McKenney - is our resident graphic designer who makes all things beautiful in their time!

These studies would not be possible without these friends who give of their time and expertise. I thank you so much!

Encouragement for you before you begin...

The book of James is one of the most practical books in the Bible. It is full of instructional wisdom on how to live a Godly life and how to grow.

If you're a Jesus-follower, don't you want to live for Him and grow your faith and spiritual life in a consistent way?

The book of James is called the 'Proverbs of the New Testament' because of its focus on wisdom, guidelines, and daily principles that will enhance your life of faith in Jesus.

James challenges all believers to live holy lives. Jesus died so that we would not continue to make sinful choices. His death and resurrected life are meant to set us free, so that we are now equipped with all that He provides and we can choose not to sin.

For this reason, the very first exercise in the book is a directed ***personal time of prayer and confession before God***. I encourage you to set aside some concentrated time to prayerfully work through this list, asking the Lord through the power and direction of His Holy Spirit, to point out anything in your life that you need to repent of and to get right with Him.

We will cover this theme of practical holiness several times in the book of James:

"But each one is tempted when he is drawn away by his own desires and enticed. Then, when desire has conceived, it gives birth to sin...." (James 1:14-15)

"Draw near to God and He will draw near to you. Cleanse your hands, you sinners; and purify your hearts...." (James 4:8)

In each week of study, you will find ***prayer starters*** based on the passage you are studying that week. Use these Biblical opportunities to pray the Scripture, asking the Lord to prepare your heart and to teach you from that passage.

You will also find declarations or ***confessions of faith*** that will be pulled directly from the passage of James that you will study each week. Take the time to say these out loud as they are pure truth taken from this highly practical book, and your faith will be built as a result.

I always love to include classic hymns and worship songs that go along with our study. This gives us an opportunity to sing our theology as we deliberately worship God each time we come to His Word to learn from Him.

I recently was reminded of this quote from missionary to China, C.T. Studd:

> ***"Only one life, will soon be past,***
> ***Only what's done for Christ will last."***

What a great theme for our study in James! So practical, but yet, so profound—just like the book of James.

My prayer for all of us as we dig in to this study is for personal growth in our spiritual lives, and an even greater sensitivity to and capacity for relationships. We will find our quest aided as we recognize through the teaching of James, the lordship of Jesus. We will be motivated as we recognize in fresh ways, how much the Lord loves us.

Jesus is the object of our faith and the One in whose Name and power we minister to others. We will see in a fresh way that Jesus is the One who rewards us as we remain steadfast in our trials, and He is the One we patiently wait for to return.

So let's all ***dare to believe together*** as we open the pages of the book of James and begin our five weeks of deeper growth!

Your sister and friend in Christ,

Marjie

Only One Life

Two little lines I heard one day,
Traveling along life's busy way;
Bringing conviction to my heart,
And from my mind would not depart;
Only one life, 'twill soon be past,
Only what's done for Christ will last.

Only one life, yes only one,
Soon will its fleeting hours be done;
Then, in 'that day' my Lord to meet,
And stand before His Judgement seat;
Only one life, 'twill soon be past,
Only what's done for Christ will last.

Only one life, the still small voice,
Gently pleads for a better choice,
Bidding me selfish aims to leave,
And to God's holy will to cleave;
Only one life, 'twill soon be past,
Only what's done for Christ will last.

Only one life, a few brief years,
Each with its burdens, hopes, and fears;
Each with its clays I must fulfill,
Living for self or in His will;
Only one life, 'twill soon be past,
Only what's done for Christ will last.

When this bright world would tempt me sore,
When Satan would a victory score;
When self would seek to have its way,
Then help me Lord with joy to say;
Only one life, 'twill soon be past,
Only what's done for Christ will last.

Give me Father, a purpose deep,
In joy or sorrow Thy word to keep;
Faithful and true what e'er the strife,
Pleasing Thee in my daily life;
Only one life, 'twill soon be past,
Only what's done for Christ will last.

Oh let my love with fervor burn,
And from the world now let me turn;
Living for Thee, and Thee alone,
Bringing Thee pleasure on Thy throne;
Only one life, 'twill soon be past,
Only what's done for Christ will last.

Only one life, yes only one,
Now let me say, "Thy will be done";
And when at last I'll hear the call,
I know I'll say " 'twas worth it all";
Only one life, 'twill soon be past,
Only what's done for Christ will last.

Only one life, 'twill soon be past,
Only what's done for Christ will last.
And when I am dying, how happy I'll be,
If the lamp of my life has been burned out for Thee.

By CT Studd

The 5 P's of Growing in Christ

A growing and maturing believer is **patient** in trials. (James 1:1-12)

A growing and maturing believer **practices** the truth. (James 2)

A growing and maturing believer has **power** over her tongue. (James 3)

A growing and maturing believer is a **peacemaker**. (James 1 and 4)

A growing and maturing believer **prays** through all troubles. (James 5)

Chapter One

"But the one who looks into the perfect law, the law of liberty, and perseveres, being no hearer who forgets but a doer who acts, he will be blessed in his doing."

James 1:25 ESV

Week 1, Day 1

Use this day to work through this list in a concentrated prayer time with the Lord (please see my personal note at the beginning of this study). Read all of the book of James if you have time. If your time is limited, read all of chapter one.

Many years ago, there was a revivalist preacher named Gypsy Smith. He was asked where revival begins. He answered: *"I draw a circle around myself and make sure everything in that circle is right with God."*

Today we will 'draw a circle' around ourselves and ask the Lord to prepare our hearts for whatever He wants to do. Revival is deeply personal and it starts at the individual level.

Today we will prepare our hearts for revival and our new study in James.

Hosea 10:12 says: *"Break up your unplowed ground; for it is time to seek the Lord, until He comes and showers righteousness on you."*

The list provided on the next few pages was authored by another old-time preacher of decades ago. He asks his readers to look to our own hearts and the spiritual ground that perhaps needs to be 'plowed up' by the Lord.

Let me tell you friends, it will take a step of *determination* to take the time to carefully go through this list before the Lord!

This list is not comfortable. This list is convicting.

But as we take the time to prayerfully sit before the Lord and ask His Holy Spirit to speak to us and convict us in any areas that need to be surrendered to Him, we will see that promised 'shower of righteousness' He speaks of in Hosea 10:12.

So, spend some time in prayer, asking the Lord to prepare your heart. Get quiet before Him and allow His Spirit to speak to your heart. It is time to seek the Lord!

Please read the message at the end of the list once you finish.

Prayer Prompts:

Ingratitude: List all the blessings and favors God has given before and after salvation. Which ones have I forgotten to thank Him for?

Losing Love for God: Consider how devastated I would be if my husband, children or other loved ones not only were lessened in their love for me, but increasingly loved someone or something else more. Is there any evidence I am lessening in my love for God?

Neglect of Bible reading: Has my Bible reading been pushed aside by an over-full schedule? As I read my Bible, am I consistently preoccupied with other things? How long has it been since reading my Bible was a delight? Do I read it so casually that I don't even remember what it said when I finish?

Neglect of Prayer: Have I substituted wishing, daydreaming, or fantasizing for real prayer? Is my faith focused on Him as I pray?

Lack of concern for the souls of others: Have I become so politically correct that I don't apply the Gospel to those I know and love? Or am I so consumed in my own life and problems, that I fail to see others around me who are desperate for Jesus, yet I am not praying for them or warning them?

Neglect of family: Am I putting myself or my needs before those of my family? What effort am I making for my family's spiritual good when it requires personal sacrifice?

Love of the world and material things: Have I allowed my love of worldly things become an idol in my heart? Am I willing to be generous with my money and possessions?

Pride: Do I have vanity about my appearance? Do I spend more time getting ready for church rather than preparing my heart and mind to worship God when I get there? Am I offended, or even slightly irritated, if others don't notice my appearance?

Envy: Do I struggle with hearing others praised? Am I jealous of those who seem more fruitful or gifted or recognizable than I am?

A critical spirit: Do I use my spirit of discernment to find fault with others who don't measure up to my standards or expectations?

Slander: Do I tell the truth with the intention of causing people to think less of another person? Whose faults, real or imagined, have I discussed behind their backs? Why have I done this?

Lack of seriousness toward God: Do I show disrespect for God by the way I sleep through my prayer time or show up late for church as though He doesn't really matter? Do I give Him the leftovers of my emotions, time, thoughts, or money?

Lying: Do I vocalize anything that is contrary to the truth? Do I design deception? What have I said that was designed to impress someone, but it wasn't the whole truth or was an exaggeration of the truth?

Cheating: Do I treat others the way I want to be treated myself? Have I stopped short of treating others the way I would want to be treated?

Hypocrisy: Do I pretend to be something or someone I am not? Am I pretending?

Robbing God: Do I spend/waste time on things that have no eternal value? Do I bring my 'whole tithe' to God as taught in His Word?

Temper: Have I lost patience with a child, co-worker, friend, spouse, or staff member? What cross words have I spoken lately? Have I lost control of my emotions, thoughts, and words so that I abuse someone else verbally? Have I lost my temper?

Hindering others: Am I respectful of other people's time, or do I take it needlessly? Have I hurt someone else's confidence because I hold them to an unreasonably high standard?

Arrogance: Do I have a tendency to accept God's forgiveness while refusing to forgive myself or someone else?

Thank you for taking the time to get quiet and alone with the Lord and allowing Him to speak to you and examine your heart. This list is meant to be between you and Him.

Perhaps you would take the time to go through it several times and allow His Spirit to continue to speak to you as you 'seek the Lord'.

The list you just worked through is meant to serve as a prompter for you to reflect and ponder your life with the Lord. It is in no way meant to be for condemnation or accusation. The Bible has made it clear that there is no condemnation for those who are in Christ Jesus.

How wonderful to know that as we confess our sins, 'He is faithful and just to forgive our sins and to cleanse us from all unrighteousness." (1 John 1:9)

Week 1, Day 2: Turning trials into joy!

Read James 1: 1-12 today and answer the questions below.

Prayer starter:

"Dear Lord, help me to learn from You today as I study James 1. Help me to count it all joy when I deal with hard things in my life. Help me to know that You are with me and for me. Grow me up in my salvation and relationship with You and help me to be complete, trusting You for fullness and wholeness. And Lord, please give me wisdom for the days ahead."

1. What are the 4 essentials for victory in our trials according to this passage? Or put another way, list out the 4 actions we are to deliberately take when we encounter trials:

   a. ______________________________ (James 1:2)

   b. ______________________________ (James 1:3)

   c. ______________________________ (James 1:4, 9-11)

   d. ______________________________ (James 1:5-8)

2. Another New Testament letter has some specific things to say about trials. Read Romans 5:3-5 and list out what you learn from this passage. Be ready to share it with your group.

3. What kind of wisdom does the Lord give to us when we ask for it according to this passage?

Bonus question: Did you learn or see anything new from your study of this passage?

Week 1, Day 3: Lord, help me to handle temptation!

Read James 1: 13-18 today and answer the questions below.

<u>Prayer Starter:</u>

"Lord, help me to learn from You today as I study this difficult passage regarding temptations. You have said in Your Word that I will be blessed if I endure temptation. You have also made it clear that You cannot and do not tempt me. Grant me spiritual sensitivity and wisdom when I am tempted, and help me to submit to You, not giving birth to sin. Help me not to be deceived."

1. What do you understand to be the 'sin process' in verses 12-16? Write it out here:

2. Take some time today to go back to the prayer prompt on Day 1. Allow the Holy Spirit to search your heart and point out anything you may need to confess.

3. The bleak news of sin is given to us in verses 12-16, then James gives us the wonderful news in verse 17. Many times, the enemy (satan) tries to trick us into believing that God is holding out on us, that He doesn't really love us or have our best interests at heart. What are the four facts we learn about the goodness of God in verse 17?

4. James used a birth analogy to talk about sin in verses 12-16. He then implies birth again in verse 18. Read this verse over several times to make sure you get the meaning of what James is explaining to us. What did God use, according to this verse, to bring us forth by? Does this increase the place and importance of God's Word in your life? Why?

Week 1, Day 4: Stop kidding yourself!

Read James 1: 19-27 today and answer the questions below.

Prayer starter:
"Dear Lord, may I be swift to hear, slow to speak and slow to anger. Help me to lay aside all things that are not of You and instead receive with meekness, the implanted Word. Help me to be a doer of the Word and not just a hearer. Help me to continue in the law of liberty and not be a forgetful hearer."

Our spiritual growth and maturity are tied directly to our relationship to God through His Word. God's Word is truth (John 17:17) and we see from this passage that we have three distinct responsibilities with God's Word if we are to grow in Him and be rightly related to others.

1. The first responsibility we have towards God's Word is to receive it. What two things did Jesus say about receiving God's Word?
    - Mark 4:24:
    - Luke 8:18:

2. In what three ways did James tell us we are to receive God's Word, in verse 19?

3. What do these 3 things mean for you personally in your walk with the Lord?

4. In verse 20, what do we see is the exact opposite of the patience God wants to produce in our lives as we mature in Christ (review James 1: 3-4)?

5. Read verse 21 again. This is a specific directive to us to prepare our hearts to receive the Word of God. James again implies an analogy here to make it easier for us to grasp. According to this verse, what are we to do in preparing our hearts to receive the Word?

6. What does meekness mean?

Week 1, Day 5: Three responsibilities towards God's Word

Read James 1: 22-27 today and answer the questions below.

Prayer Starter:

"Dear Lord, help me in my pursuit of You to be one who readily receives Your Word. Help me to have a prepared heart that daily receives Your Word with meekness and joy."

Yesterday, we learned that our spiritual growth and maturity as believers are tied directly to our relationship with God through His Word. One of three responsibilities we have towards God's Word is to ***receive*** it.

The second responsibility we have towards God's Word is to ***practice*** it.

1. It's not enough to just hear the Word, according to verse 22, what else is necessary for our growth in Christ?

2. What does being a 'doer of the Word' mean to you and what does it look like?

3. Earlier in the passage, James compared the Word of God to seed (v. 21), but in verses 23-24, what analogy does James use for the Word of God?

4. Which three mistakes does James mention that people often do when approaching the Word of God, in verse 24?

5. Why did James call the Word of God, in verse 25, the 'perfect law of liberty'? What does that mean to you?

6. A third responsibility we have towards the Word of God is to ***share*** it. Read verses 26-27 again. James mentions religion here and explains that its meaning is the practicing of God's Word and sharing it with others. List out the three ways growing believers demonstrate their 'religion' or the sharing of God's Word:

Biblical Confessions from James 1:

- I can count it all joy when I encounter trials because I know my faith in Jesus will produce patience in me.
- When I need wisdom, I ask the Lord for it, and He gives it to me in vast amounts as I trust Him.
- When I face temptation, I cry out to God for help and deliverance.
- Every good and perfect gift comes from the Father.
- I desire to be a doer of the Word and not just a hearer, this prevents me from being deceived.
- The Word of God is my direct source of freedom.
- I desire to share the Word of God through my speech, my service to others, and by keeping myself unspotted from the world.

Great is Thy Faithfulness

Great is Thy faithfulness, O God my Father,
There is no shadow of turning with Thee;
Thou changest not, Thy compassions they fail not;
As Thou has been Thou forever wilt be.

Great is Thy faithfulness! Great is Thy faithfulness!
Morning by morning new mercies I see;
All I have needed Thy hand hath provided;
Great is Thy faithfulness, Lord, unto me!

Summer and winter, and springtime and harvest,
Sun, moon, and stars in their courses above,
Join with all nature in manifold witness,
To Thy great faithfulness, mercy, and love.

Great is Thy faithfulness! Great is Thy faithfulness!
Morning by morning new mercies I see;
All I have needed Thy hand hath provided;
Great is Thy faithfulness, Lord, unto me!

Pardon for sin and a peace that endureth,
Thy own dear presence to cheer and to guide;
Strength for today and bright hope for tomorrow,
Blessings all mine, with ten thousand beside!

Great is Thy faithfulness! Great is Thy faithfulness!
Morning by morning new mercies I see;
All I have needed Thy hand hath provided;
Great is Thy faithfulness, Lord, unto me!

Thomas O. Chisholm; William Runyan
1923

Chapter Two

'If you really fulfill the royal law according to the Scripture, "You shall love your neighbor as yourself," you are doing well.'

James 2:8 ESV

Week 2, Day 1: A mature Christian practices the truth.

Read James 2:1-13 today and answer the questions below.

Prayer starter:
"Lord, as I come to your Word today, continue to prepare my heart to receive it. Point out anything in me that does not glorify You. May I never be one who holds the faith of Jesus with partiality. Help me never to judge by outward appearances or to dishonor others. For the glory of Your Name, I pray."

Last week we learned there are three distinct responsibilities we have towards the Word of God:

- Receive the Word
- Practice the Word
- Share the Word

In James 2, our study takes us deeper into the practice of the truth of God's Word with additional practical aspects of walking it out as it relates to others.

1. From this passage, what are some specific things James teaches that result from showing partiality? List them here.

2. Jesus taught on this same principle. Read Luke 14:7-14 and write out things you learn from Jesus Himself.

3. What is the 'royal law' of the Bible?

4. Think of a time in your life when you were not favored. How did you respond/react? Have you forgiven those who offended you and quite possibly rejected you? Spend some time today, if needed, praying about this issue.

Week 2, Day 2: Beware of personal favoritism

Read James 2:1-13 today and answer the questions below.

__Prayer Starter:__

"Dear Lord, as I dive deeper into your standards for treating people according to the royal law of Scripture, enable me by Your Spirit to be consistent in all of my relationships—seeing each person I meet as made in the image of You, Lord. May I practice the lordship of Jesus in all of my relationships, and may I bring glory to Your Name."

1. Read Genesis 1:26 and Acts 17:26-29. In light of these two additional Scripture passages, write out a Biblical position on no partiality.

2. How do we practice the lordship of Jesus Christ in our human relationships? Get real and practical with your answer!

3. Last week, we learned that true 'religion' is practicing God's Word and sharing it with others. In light of that definition and what you've studied so far this week, explain this statement: **Empty religion will betray itself in relationships.**

Week 2, Day 3: A difficult passage....

Read James 2:10-13 today and answer the questions below.

Prayer starter:

"Lord, this book of James is sometimes hard to understand and to grasp exactly what it means for me today. Grant me wisdom to understand Your Word. Lord, increase my faith! And may the reality of my faith be reflected in how I treat Your Word and how I treat others."

1. What did Jesus say in John 5:24 and Paul in Romans 8:1, regarding Christian believers and their sins?

2. Since James, the author, spent so much time with Jesus while He was on the earth, this book reflects the teaching he heard and received with his own ears from the Lord Himself! Most notable and remarkable is how the book of James mirrors Jesus' Sermon on the Mount. Read the following passages from that famous sermon and tell how these principles relate to James 2:10-13.

   Read:

   - Matthew 5:21-26

   - Matthew 5:33-37

   - Matthew 7:1-5

   - Matthew 7:21-23

3. What are your conclusions from your personal study of this passage when compared with other Scriptures?

One obvious conclusion from this passage is: **our beliefs should control and impact our behavior.** If we really believe that Jesus is the Son of God, that His Word is absolutely true, and one day we will stand before Him and give an answer for our works, then our lives and relationships will display our convictions.

Mercy and justice both come from God. They do not cancel each other out. When God finds repentance and faith, His justice enables Him to show mercy. Where He finds rebellion and unbelief, His justice demands that He respond accordingly.

For more of Jesus' teaching on this, please read Matthew 18: 21-35.

As we tackle this difficult section of verses, I hope you recognize why we started out our study in James with the deliberate time of drawing near to God in prayer, asking Him to examine our hearts and to cleanse us of anything we need to confess and repent of.

Mercy triumphs over judgment!

Week 2, Day 4: Faith without works is dead

Read James 2:14-26 today and answer the questions below.

Prayer Starter:
"Lord, help me to understand the type of faith that pleases You. Faith is not simply an idea that is separate from real life. Help me to live a life of faith that collaborates with my works. Help me to be inspired by those who have gone before me and pointed me towards a greater faith—like Abraham and Rahab. Teach me from Your Word today."

1. From this passage in James, write out the things you learn about faith and works.

2. Faith is a key doctrine in the Christian life. Look up the following passages and write out truths given about our faith in Christ:

   - Ephesians 2:8-9:

   - 2 Corinthians 5:7:

   - Hebrews 11:6:

   - Romans 14:23:

3. According to James 2:18, what do our works reveal?

4. In James 2:19, what kind of faith is described?

Week 2, Day 5: Dynamic and living faith

Read James 2:14-26 again today and answer the questions below.

Prayer Starter:
"Dear Lord, I want my faith to be a living and dynamic faith, revealing itself in loving works and acts and words towards others. Help me not to look to my actions as my confidence, but instead, help my daily faith to be based on Your Word—a faith that is real, resulting from a changed life through Jesus Christ my Lord."

1. James asks the believer the question in verse 22: "Do you see that faith was ***working together*** with his works, and by works faith was made perfect?"

   The Greek for ***working together*** is sunergeo—we get our modern word, ***synergy*** from it. It means to cooperate, to help, to collaborate, to co-labor. There is a practical harmony or synergy between our vertical faith in God and our horizontal works to a needy world. In other words, our faith is both spiritual and practical.

   Read Abraham's story of faith and write out your observations as it relates to our James passage: Genesis 15:6; Genesis 22:1-18.

2. Summarize what you have learned from James 2, and come prepared to share your insights with your group this week in our gathering.

As we conclude this chapter on faith and works, here's another opportunity to examine our hearts before God:

1. Have I honestly realized I am a sinner and admitted and confessed this to God?
2. Have I ever seriously been alarmed over my sins?
3. Do I truly understand that Jesus Christ died for my sins and rose again, enabling me to live a life of faith and obedience for Him?
4. Have I confessed that I cannot save myself?
5. Have I trusted Christ and Christ alone for my salvation?
6. Do I sincerely and consistently repent of my sins when I become aware of them?
7. Do I secretly enjoy my sin in any way?
8. Do I enjoy a living relationship with Jesus through His Word and by His Spirit?
9. Has there been an obvious change in my life since Jesus came into it and took over?
10. Do I consistently display good works as an outworking of my faith in Jesus, or are my works occasional and not effective?
11. Can others see Jesus in me?
12. Do I have a desire to share Jesus with others, or am I ashamed of Him in any way?
13. Do I enjoy the fellowship of God's people?
14. Is worship a delight to me?
15. Am I ready for the Lord's return if He were to come today?

<u>Biblical confessions from James 2:</u>

- By the grace of God, I will not hold the faith of my Lord Jesus Christ, the Lord of glory, with partiality.
- Through Jesus, I will speak and do as one who is judged by the law of liberty.
- Mercy triumphs over judgment.
- Jesus enables my faith to be synergized with my works.
- Through Jesus, my saving faith produces obedience and joy.

Trust and Obey

When we walk with the Lord,
In the light of His word,
What a glory He sheds on our way!
Let us do His good will;
He abides with us still,
And with all who will trust and obey.
Trust and obey, for there's no other way
To be happy in Jesus, but to trust and obey.

Not a burden we bear,
Not a sorrow we share,
But our toil He doth richly repay;
Not a grief or a loss,
Not a frown or a cross,
But is blest if we trust and obey.
Trust and obey, for there's no other way
To be happy in Jesus, but to trust and obey.

But we never can prove,
The delights of His love,
Until all on the altar we lay;
For the favor He shows,
And the joy He bestows,
Are for them who will trust and obey.
Trust and obey, for there's no other way
To be happy in Jesus, but to trust and obey.

Then in fellowship sweet,
We will sit at His feet,
Or we'll walk by His side in the way;
What He says we will do,
Where He sends we will go,
Never fear, only trust and obey.
Trust and obey, for there's no other way
To be happy in Jesus, but to trust and obey

John H. Sammis; Daniel B. Towner

Chapter Three

"Who is wise and understanding among you?
By his good conduct let him show his works
in the meekness of wisdom."

James 3:13 ESV

Week 3, Day 1: The world's smallest troublemaker: the untameable tongue!

Read James 3:1-12 today and answer the questions below.

Prayer Starter:

"Lord as I come to Your Word for today and study what You say about the tongue and the potential damage or blessing it can do, please speak to me specifically through Your Word. Help me to truly understand how the tongue is a rudder, a fire, a beast, but if my tongue is submitted to You, I can be a blessing---a spring of fresh water to others. Help me, Jesus!"

1. So far, we have learned from James two characteristics of a mature believer: she is patient in trials (James 1), and she practices the truth (James 2). In James 3, we see a third character quality of a mature believer: she has power over her tongue.

   From this passage, list out the six pictures of the tongue that James gives to us:

2. Apparently, everyone that James addresses in this letter wanted to teach and be a spiritual leader, so James had to issue them a warning. Write out the specifics of James' warning to the believers here:

3. Look up these additional passages of Scripture that directly address the tongue and summarize what each one means:

   - Proverbs 18:21:

   - Psalm 141:3:

   - Matthew 12:34:

4. How do the ‘bit’ and the ‘rudder’ affect the lives of others, according to this passage?

Week 3, Day 2: The tongue has the power to destroy

Read James 3:1-12 again today and answer the questions below.

<u>Prayer Starter:</u>
"Dear Lord, I want my tongue to be a source of life and health for others. I have seen from Your Word that my tongue has the power to bring life or to bring death. I ask You to set a watch over the door of my lips and remind me that what comes out of my mouth, reveals what's really in my heart. Continue to teach me today out of Your Word and help me to grow more mature in my faith and walk with You."

1. In verses 5-8 of this passage, list out what you learn specifically as to the type of damage our tongues can do.

2. As you have studied so far, has the Lord brought anything to mind that you need to confess or go and make right with someone else with regard to your tongue? Take the time to remedy that situation now if He has.

3. Look up the following verses and relate them back to this passage in James. Summarize the lessons you learn from them:
    - Proverbs 26: 20-21
    - Psalm 39: 1, 3
    - Proverbs 14:29
    - Proverbs 17:27
    - Colossians 4:6

Week 3, Day 3: The tongue has the power to delight

Read James 3: 1-12 again today and answer the questions below.

<u>Prayer Starter:</u>
"Dear Lord, Your Word tells me in James that 'out of the same mouth proceed blessing and cursing.' I want my mouth to be known as one that continually brings blessing everywhere I go and into every arena I enter. May You, Lord, be pleased with my daily speech."

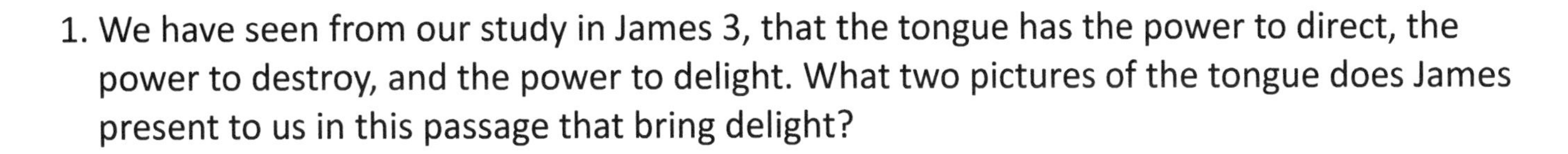

1. We have seen from our study in James 3, that the tongue has the power to direct, the power to destroy, and the power to delight. What two pictures of the tongue does James present to us in this passage that bring delight?

2. A fountain provides cool and refreshing water. Water is what we all need to stay alive. Look up the following verses on water and relate them to this passage on the tongue:

    - Proverbs 18:4

    - Proverbs 10:11

    - Proverbs 13: 14

    - Proverbs 12:18

    - Romans 15:32

    - John 15:3

    - Ephesians 5:26-27

3. The tongue is also compared to a tree. Trees are vitally important to our soil as they hold it down; they provide beauty and shade, and they bear fruit. Our tongues, our speech, can provide metaphorical shelter and shade to others who are weary and worn out. Jesus said, "The words that I speak unto you, they are spirit, and they are life." (John 6:63). As we conclude this lesson on the tongue, list out ways the words of others have been a source of refreshment and life for you. Also list out any ways that you have specifically encouraged others lately.

Bonus activity:
Take the time to write a note or email to someone who has recently spoken words of life to you. Let them know how you were specifically encouraged by what they said. Use some of the verses from this study to build them up in their faith. By doing this activity, you are maturing in your faith, and you are demonstrating practical (real) Christian faith.

Week 3, Day 4: Where to get wisdom

Read James 3: 13-18 today and answer the questions below.

Prayer Starter:

"Dear Lord, thank You for Your Word which is an infinite source of wisdom for Your followers. I long to be wise and to be growing in wisdom. Thank You for instructing me to just ask You for wisdom when I need it. I want to be one of those who is counted as wise and understanding like You mention in James 3. I want to show this by my good conduct and works done in the meekness of wisdom."

1. What are the evidences of false wisdom?

2. What are the evidences of true wisdom?

3. Verse 18 tells us how the 'fruit of righteousness' is sown. Tell what that means in your own words and bring other Scriptures in to confirm your answer.

Week 3, Day 5: The fruit of wisdom

Read James 3: 13-18 again today and answer the questions below.

<u>Prayer starter:</u>
"Lord, grow in me true, spiritual wisdom. I long to live a life that bears the fruit of righteousness sown in peace. May Jesus shine brightly in me each day."

1. Yesterday we pulled out from this passage, the evidences of true wisdom. Here is the list, along with some additional passages to look up and write out, expanding your understanding of the evidences. Look up these verses and write out what you learn:

    - Meekness: Galatians 5:23; James 3:3

    - Purity: 2 Corinthians 11:3

    - Peace: Isaiah 32:17

    - Gentleness: Galatians 5:23

    - Agreeable: James 1:19

    - Mercy: Luke 6:36; Luke 10:25-37

- Good fruits: John 15:1-16

- Decisiveness: James 1:6

- Sincerity: Ephesians 4:15

2. Which one of these qualities really jumped out to you? Which one (or ones) will you commit to pray into, asking the Lord to further mature and develop you in this area?

Biblical confessions from James 3:

- By the grace of God and through the power of the Holy Spirit, I submit my tongue to the Lord, longing to bless God and bring a blessing to others.
- My tongue shall be a fountain of fresh water and a fruitful tree, and will bring joy and encouragement to others, as I walk in the power of the Holy Spirit.
- I will be wise and understanding as I obey and trust God in the meekness of wisdom.
- The Holy Spirit will equip me with wisdom that is from above displaying gentleness, peace, mercy, and good fruits.
- By the power of the Holy Spirit, I will sow the fruit of righteousness as I make peace.

For additional study:

If you want to develop a more expanded list of Biblical confessions that cover various topics, this is provided for you to do along with this study or upon its completion. This would be a great exercise/study to do with other friends if you still wanted to gather after our study is finished. It is a fruitful exercise to take you even deeper into the Word of God and to strengthen and build your faith.

Example: "I thank You Lord that you have given me wisdom that is from above and it is pure, peaceable, gentle, willing to yield, full of mercy & good fruits, without partiality and without hypocrisy." (Jas. 3:17)

Anxiety & Worry: Deut. 31:6; Ps 86:7; Prov. 15:15; Matt. 6:27, 31, 33; Mark 4:19; Phi.4:6-7; 1 Pet. 5:7

Believer's Authority: Matt. 16:19; Matt. 28:18-19; Eph. 1:20-22 & Eph. 2:6; James 4:7

Parenting: Deut.28:13; Deut.30:19-20; Prov. 17:6; Prov. 31:28; 2Cor. 6:14; Gal.5:16; Eph.1:17-18

Confessing the Word: Josh.1:8; Ps.119:105; Is.48:6-7; Is.55:11; Jer.1:12; Rom.4:17; Heb.4:12,14

Contentment: Ps 16:6; Ps. 17:15; Ps. 84:10; Ps. 92:4-5; Ps. 107:8-9; Phil. 4:19; 1Tim. 6:6-8

God with me: Ps. 3:3; Ps. 34:15,17; Ps. 40:1-3; Ps. 42:6, 8, 11; 2Cor. 7:6; 1Pet. 5:6-7

Discouragement: Ps. 3:3; Ps. 30:11-12; John 10:10; John 16:33; Romans 8:28; 2Cor. 1:4

Faith: Hab.2:4; Matt.17:20; Mark 11:23; Romans 3:28; Romans 10:17; Romans 15:13; Gal.3:24-25

Fear: Ps.23:4; Ps.27:1; Ps.91:4-5; Prov.29:25; Is.41:10; 2Tim.1:7; Heb. 13:5-6; 1Pet.3:14; 1Jn. 4:18

Forgiveness: Matt. 6:14; Mark 11:25-26; Romans 4:7-8; Eph. 4:32; Col. 3:13; Luke 6:37

Grace: Ps. 84:11; Luke 2:40; Acts 13:43; Romans 5:15, 20-21; Eph 2:8; James 4:6

Healing: Ps. 30:2; Ps. 103:3; Ps. 107:20; Ps. 118:17; Ps. 147:3; James 5:14-15; IPet. 2:24

Loneliness: Ps. 25:16; Ps. 27:10; Ps. 46:1; Isa. 41:10; Matt. 28:20; John 14:18; 2Cor. 6:18

Finances: Deut. 8:18; Deut. 28:8,11; Ps. 1:3; Ps. 34:10; Malachi 3:10; Matt. 6:3-4; Matt. 6:19-21

Create in me a Clean Heart

Create in me a clean heart, oh God
And renew a right spirit within me
Create in me a clean heart, oh God
And renew a right spirit within me

Cast me not away from Thy presence, oh Lord
Take not Thy Holy Spirit from me
Restore unto me the joy of Thy salvation
And renew a right spirit within me

Keith Green

Chapter Four

"Submit yourselves therefore to God. Resist the devil, and he will flee from you. Draw near to God, and he will draw near to you. Cleanse your hands, you sinners, and purify your hearts, you double-minded."

James 4:7-8 ESV

Week 4, Day 1: War…what is it good for?

Read James 4: 1-10 today and answer the questions below.

Prayer Starter:
"Lord, as I come to Your Word today, I ask You to show me anything in my life that is keeping me from growing closer to You. As I study about pride and strife and compromising with the world and its system, show me specifically from Your Word, what I need to see, hear, and learn. May I leave this time of study today, more mature in my walk with You and my understanding of Your Word and Your standards for life."

1. What does James say in verses 1-2 causes war and arguments with others?

James begins this section of his letter with a discussion of disagreements and arguing. As we read the New Testament, we discover that some of the early churches had more than their share of disagreements and fights among each other!

James mentions several types of disagreements among Christians:

- Church fights: James 1:19-20 and James 3:13-18
- Rich vs. poor: James 2:1-9
- Personal fights: James 4:11-12
- Employment struggles: James 5:1-6

Why are we at war with each other when we belong to the same 'family'? We are brothers and sisters in Christ. We 'play for the same team' and we are not competing with each other! We even have the Holy Spirit living inside of us to help us navigate difficult situations.

James explains this all by breaking down the 'war' we fight into two components. We will be studying each one of these this week as we dive into James 4. Here's how James explains it to us so that we understand through the Word what/who we are dealing with and how best to walk in victory, peace and love:

- We are at war with ourselves: James 4:1-3
- We are at war with God: James 4:4-10

2. If you could sum up the main cause of sin (war) in verses 1-3, what one word would you use?

3. In the context of being at war with ourselves, how would you explain this statement: 'When our praying is wrong, our whole Christian life is wrong.'?

4. Even though we've just looked at 3 verses today, what new insight did you learn from this perspective in James, and how will this insight equip you in the war with yourself?

Week 4, Day 2: At war with God

Read James 4:4-10 today and answer the questions below.

Prayer Starter:
"Lord, I draw near to You today and I submit to You. Thank you for Your Word which is the answer for all of life. Speak to me out of it today and lead me along the path of everlasting life."

1. What is the number one thing, according to verse 4, that causes us to be at enmity with God?

The 'world' refers to the word system with its values, mind-set, philosophies of life, and priorities that run contrary to the ways and heart of God. Friendship with the world can cause us to neglect the nurturing of our relationship with God.

2. The Scriptures give us insight on how to do battle in this arena. Look up each verse and write out what you learn:

- 1 John 2:15-16:

- 1 John 4:4:

- 1 John 5:19:

- Mark 8:36:

- Romans 12:2:

- Philippians 2:5:

- Titus 3:5:

3. What are some things that you have recently battled that have sought to lure you away from your relationship with the Lord? How has the Lord helped you in the battle and what have you learned?

Week 4, Day 3: A strategy for life

Read James 4: 4-10 today and answer the questions below.

Prayer Starter:

"Dear Lord, today I choose to stand on the truth and promises of Your Word. I long to be equipped for daily battle in my life. I want to learn and know and respond by using the spiritual strategies You have provided in Your Word that equip and enable me to continue to press in to You as I rely on Your Holy Spirit, Your abundant grace, Your ever-present nearness. Thank You Lord, for being with me and for me."

From James we have seen two battlefronts: war with ourselves and war with God. The world and its systems seek to draw us away from our relationship with the Lord, but there is another force that seeks to lure us away as well.

1. According to verse 7, who are we to resist?

2. In verses 5-7, we are told of three different 'helps' the Lord gives to us as we seek to resist the enemy. What are they?

3. If you could summarize verse 7 into a simple strategy for the Christian life, what would it be?

4. What 3-pronged plan can you draw out from verses 7-10 with regard to cultivating peace in your relationship with the Lord?

5. James gives some pretty hard words to us in verses 8 and 9. He does this because he wants us to know that it is possible to submit outwardly to God but ignore what is really going on with us inwardly. It is possible to take our sins lightly and to even laugh about it. "Oh, I know I have a terrible temper. That's just the way I am."

   James wants us all to realize that sin is serious, and a distinguishing mark of humility is facing our sin and disobedience head on. Look up the following Scriptures that give credence to James' warnings here:

   - Proverbs 6:16-17—what does God hate?

   - Psalm 51:17—what does God desire?

   - Isaiah 66:2—who does God look to?

   - Psalm 34:18—who is God near to?

Week 4, Day 4: Don't judge a brother & don't boast about tomorrow

Read James 4:11-17 today and answer the questions below.

Prayer Starter:

"Dear Lord, so many times I have fallen short of Your standards. Today I draw near to You. I rely on Your precious Holy Spirit to guide and direct me into Your truth as presented in Your Word. I ask You to give me a heart for You and one that longs to stay in consistent fellowship, seeking Your will and hearing Your voice."

1. Verse 11 has definite instruction as to how we are to relate to our brothers and sisters in Christ. Write out the specifics here, and then look up what Jesus had to say about it in Matthew 7:1-5.

2. According to verses 13-16, what should our approach, attitude and outlook be toward the future? Write out the specifics here.

3. James finishes this section with another reminder about sin. Write out the two aspects of sin that we all need to pay careful attention to in our lives.

Week 4, Day 5: A final review

Prayer Starter:
"Lord, as we draw near to the end of this study in James, take the time I will spend with You today and bring to my remembrance anything I have glossed over or missed. I do not want to be at war with You or with others. I want to walk in daily fellowship with You, hearing Your voice and doing Your will, all for Your glory."

Today is a great day for review!

If you feel you need the time to 'marinate' in James chapter 4, please do so for your study time allotted today.

If you feel you did your due diligence this week, go back and highlight the lessons from earlier weeks that have meant the most to you by reviewing the following:

- Read the entire book of James today and use a red pencil to underline the verses that really speak to you.
- Go back through each day's homework with a yellow highlighter and reflect on those questions or scriptures that had great impact on your heart and life.
- Go through each week's Biblical confessions and say them all out loud again today.
- Follow through on anything the Holy Spirit brings to mind that you need to pray about or do.
- Write a note of encouragement to anyone the Lord brings to mind.

Biblical confessions from James 4:

- Thank You, Lord, for the Holy Spirit who dwells in me.
- I am standing in Your abundant grace, Lord, as I submit to You and resist the devil.
- You, Lord, draw near to me as I draw near to You.
- Thank you for lifting me up, Lord, as I humble myself in Your sight.

Higher Ground

I'm pressing on the upward way,
New heights I'm gaining every day;
Still praying as I'm onward bound,
"Lord, plant my feet on higher ground."

Refrain:
Lord, lift me up and let me stand,
By faith, on Heaven's tableland,
A higher plane than I have found;
Lord, plant my feet on higher ground.

My heart has no desire to stay
Where doubts arise and fears dismay;
Though some may dwell where those abound,
My prayer, my aim, is higher ground.

I want to live above the world,
Though Satan's darts at me are hurled;
For faith has caught the joyful sound,
The song of saints on higher ground.

I want to scale the utmost height
And catch a gleam of glory bright;
But still I'll pray till heav'n I've found,
"Lord, plant my feet on higher ground."

Johnson Oatman, Jr; Charles H. Gabriel

Chapter Five

"The prayer of a righteous person
has great power as it is working."

James 5:16

Week 5, Day 1: Rich oppressors will be judged

Read all of James 5 today and answer the questions below.

<u>Prayer Starter:</u>
"Lord, as I come to the end of this deliberate time of study in James, I ask You to remind me of the lessons I've gleaned so far. Keep me mindful of the context of the entire book. Speak to me specifically out of chapter 5 and show me what I need to learn, apply, and do—especially with regard to patience in trials and prayer."

This is a good time to review the five over-arching themes of the book of James as we wrap up:

The 5 P's of Growing in Christ

- A growing and maturing believer is ***patient*** in trials. (James 1 & James 5)
- A growing and maturing believer ***practices*** the truth. (James 2)
- A growing and maturing believer has ***power*** over her tongue. (James 3)
- A growing and maturing believer is a ***peacemaker***. (James 1 & 4)
- A growing and maturing believer ***prays*** through all troubles. (James 5)

1. In verses 1-6, James has some difficult things to say to rich people. It is important to keep in mind the context of James' letter. In those days, there was no middle class; people were either rich or poor. James is specifically speaking to those rich people who are oppressing the poor and who acquired their wealth by illegal means. From these verses, what do you learn about how we are to use our wealth?

2. According to verses 1-6, what were some specific ways the rich were oppressing the poor? List them out here.

3. Have you seen this played out in our current culture and society? What practical lessons can you personally glean from this section?

4. What should be the Biblical response to the poor among us?

Week 5, Day 2: Be patient and persevering

Read James 5: 7-12 today and answer the questions below.

__Prayer Starter:__

"Lord, thank You for this specific instruction out of this section in James. I need Your help and the power of the Holy Spirit to be patient and to not grumble against my brothers and sisters in Christ. Would You, Lord, establish my heart? And teach me more about what that means and what part I have in that. Remind me that I am blessed as I endure."

1. What personal things is the Lord saying to you out of this section given your current circumstances? Write these down and then put them in a form of a prayer, submitting them to God and trusting in Him to help you and to take care of all things that concern you.

2. James provides another picture for us in this section: a farmer. List out some of the jobs of a farmer and compare this to being a 'spiritual farmer'. Why does a farmer willingly wait so long?

3. In verse 8, James gives the word to us that we are to establish our hearts. What does that mean? What are some specific ways that our hearts get established? Is your heart currently being established? If so, how?

4. "Do not grumble against one another...." How are you doing with this one? Why do you think this command is listed in this section on patience? (Spend some time praying on this one if you need to.)

Week 5, Day 3: Patience continued...

Read James 5: 7-12 today and answer the questions below.

Prayer Starter:

"Lord, just as the title of this day is called 'patience continued', I ask You to continue to develop in me a patient heart and a patient spirit. Help me to trust You, to believe You, to know that You love me, and You have my best interests at heart."

1. "Take the prophets..." (verse 10): James' audience of Jewish Christians would have understood this simple reference. When Jesus preached His famous Sermon on the Mount, He also referenced the prophets as an example of victory over persecution. Look up the following verses and next to each one, write a summary of what you glean from other passages that confirm James' teachings here:

   - Matthew 5:10-12:

   - 2 Timothy 3:12:

   - Romans 15:4:

2. A book was out almost three decades ago entitled, ***A Long Obedience in the Same Direction***. It was a book about discipleship in our instant society.

   The story of Job and his trials most certainly personifies this. Take some time to reflect on the life of Job—the specific Old Testament example of perseverance given to us by James. The ideal would be to read the entire book of Job, but if you cannot, look up the following verses and write out the lessons you specifically learn from Job's life and responses:

   - Job 1: 21 & 22:

- Job 2: 10:

- Job 42:10:

3. In verse 12, James gives another directive to us for our daily lives. What are some practical ways that you can be doer of this Biblical command? Read also Matthew 5:34-37 to see what Jesus had to say about this very thing.

Week 5, Day 4: Let's pray

Read James 5:13-20 and answer the questions.

<u>Prayer Starter:</u>
"Lord, thank You for giving me the high and holy privilege of prayer. Thank You for giving me direct access to You. Thank you for listening and answering according to Your good and perfect will. Help me to trust You when I don't see answers coming right away. Help me to persevere and to be patient."

"We participate in the reign of Christ through prayer....in Him we then find ourselves at the very seat of government." (Swiss Theologian, Karl Barth)

"Imagine that the President of the United States calls your cell phone...as you recover from the shock, he calmly explains that, in the interests of greater democracy, the government has decided to include the opinions of an ordinary, representative citizen in certain important decisions relating to national security. Your name has been chosen. He therefore asks if you would be willing to come and sit with his executive to share your unique thoughts, insights, and opinions on behalf of the people. I'm pretty sure that although you might be nervous, you would find the time, in fact, you would cancel anything to attend. It would be one of the greatest honors of your life.

As a Christian, you have received an even greater invitation. The King of Kings requests your presence at the very seat of government. He offers you a place....so that you can influence through prayer. It is an unspeakable honor, and yet we are often too busy, or too disbelieving to accept the invitation."

-Peter Grieg, Dirty Glory: Go where your best prayers take you, page 105

As we wrap up our study in the book of James, we will take the next two days to focus on prayer. James encouraged us to pray and provides four types of situations in which God answers our prayers:

- Prayer for the suffering-James 5:13
- Prayer for the sick-James 5:14-16
- Prayer for the nation-James 5:17-18
- Prayer for the straying brother or sister in Christ-James 5:19-20

1. According to verse 13, what are we to do when we encounter suffering or a trying circumstance?

2. How does James 4:6 fit into this command to pray?

3. How does singing fit within this command to pray and what does our singing reveal about our spiritual lives?

4. In verse 14, who is to call for the elders of the church to pray?

5. Read Mark 6:13 for another reference on prayer. Using this reference and others you are familiar with, explain why oil is used during these prayer times.

Week 5, Day 5: Let's keep praying

Read James 5: 13-20 again today and answer the questions below.

Prayer Starter:

"Lord, thank You for showing us through James 5 that You care about everything in our lives, and You encourage us to bring it all to You in prayer. May Your glorious will be done in my life."

1. James does not provide a blanket formula for prayer or for the prayer for healing. In verse 15, what can be a possible cause of a person's sickness?

2. What practical 'doing' (remember to be a doer of the Word) does James call for in verse 16? How are these two things important for maturing in our relationship with Jesus?

3. Based on Elijah's example in verses 17-18, how are we to pray? What encourages you out of these 2 verses? How will this impact your own personal prayer life? (If you want the background on this story, you can read 1 Kings 17-18). How will you apply this to pray for our nation?

4. James turns the focus from affliction, sickness, and national need to the restoration of a brother or sister who is not following or obeying the Lord in verses 19-20. This person has 'wandered from the truth', and the truth means the Word of God. Unless a Christian stays close to the truth, he or she will start to drift away. This is why a daily reading of God's Word is so important for our spiritual health and maturity. Write out what our response is to be towards a wandering brother or sister in Christ.

5. This brings us to the end of our study of James, where the emphasis has been on spiritual maturity. This is an opportune time to examine our hearts once again in light of God's Word and all we have studied throughout these weeks together. Here are a few questions you can use as prayer starters or prompts as you take a few minutes to reflect on the truth of God's Word through the book of James:

   - Am I becoming more and more patient in the trials and hardships of my life?
   - Do I actively resist temptation, or do I go right up to the line and play with it?
   - Do I fid joy in the Word of God? Does it have prominence in my life?
   - Is my life saturated with the Word of God, affecting and transforming my thinking, my talking, and my living?
   - Do I practice the truth of God's Word on a daily basis and am I growing in this?
   - Do I have power over my tongue?
   - Am I a peacemaker rather than a troublemaker or a divider?
   - Am I a friend of God or am I a friend of the world?
   - Do I make my plans and then just ask God to bless them? Or do I consider God's will ahead of my own?
   - Do I honor God with my income?
   - Am I selfish with my money?
   - Do I faithfully pay my bills on time?
   - Do I have debt that I should take care of and prioritize?
   - Is my first response prayer whenever I encounter any trouble or something unexpected?
   - Do others seek me out for prayer support?
   - Do I seek to restore my wandering brother or sister, or do I gossip about them instead?

Biblical declarations from James 5:

- The Lord of Hosts hears my cry.
- I patiently wait for Him to answer my prayers and this establishes my heart in Him.
- I am blessed as I persevere.
- I pray whenever I have needs and trials, and I sing for joy in the midst.
- My effective and fervent prayer will avail much.
- I will pray for healing and deliverance and will join my faith with others in prayer.

Hills and Valleys

I've walked among the shadows
You wiped my tears away
And I've felt the pain of heartbreak
And I've seen the brighter days
And I've prayed prayers to heaven from my lowest place
And I have held the blessings
God, you give and take away
No matter what I have, Your grace is enough
No matter where I am, I'm standing in Your love

On the mountains, I will bow my life
To the one who set me there
In the valley, I will lift my eyes to the one who sees me there
When I'm standing on the mountain aft, didn't get there on my own
When I'm walking through the valley end, no I am not alone!
You're God of the hills and valleys!
Hills and Valleys!
God of the hills and valleys
And I am not alone!

I've watched my dreams get broken
In You I hope again!
No matter what I know
Know I'm safe inside Your hand

On the mountains, I will bow my life
To the one who set me there
In the valley, I will lift my eyes to the one who sees me there
When I'm standing on the mountain aft, didn't get there on my own
When I'm walking through the valley end, no I am not alone!
You're God of the hills and valleys!
Hills and Valleys!
God of the hills and valleys
And I am not alone!

Father, you give and take away
Every joy and every pain
Through it all you will remain
Over it all!

Songwriters: CHUCK BUTLER,JONATHAN LINDLEY SMITH,TAUREN WELLS

Works Cited

The Amplified Bible, La Habra, CA: The Lockman Foundation, 2015. Print.

The Hymnal for Worship and Celebration, Waco, TX. Word Music. 1986

The New Spirit-Filled Life Bible. Nashville, TN. Thomas Nelson Publishers, 2002. Print

The Wiersbe Bible Commentary. Colorado Springs, CO.
David C. Cook Publishing, 2007. Print.

Greig, Peter. "Dirty Glory; Go where your best prayers take you." NavPress, 2016. Print.

paulhockley.com/2016/05/24/quote-only-one-life-twill-soon-be-past-poem-by-c-t-studd/

Additional lyrics from:

lyricsmode.com/lyrics/k/keith_green/create_in_me_a_clean_heart.html

www.metrolyrics.com/hills-and-valleys-lyrics-tauren-wells.htm

About the Author

Marjie Schaefer believes the Word of God is relevant, powerful, transformational, and life-giving to every single human being on the planet. She has spent her adult life investing in others and inviting them to join her in this pursuit of deeper truth.

As a result of her passion and pursuit, she has spent many years teaching women of all ages how to dig into the Word of God, and how to mine the treasures of it for themselves. She started in college and has continued on as a wife and mom, opening her heart and home to those who hunger and thirst for more of God and His Word in their lives.

Marjie and her team currently lead the ministry, ***Flourish Through the Word***, which is a community of women in the greater Seattle region committed to being equipped through God's Word. As a result of their time together in the Word, the women then move out into their arenas of influence, shining their lights for Jesus. You can find out more about this ministry and upcoming events and Bible studies at ***FlourishThroughTheWord.com.*** You can also find them on Facebook: ***Flourish Through the Word Ministries.***

Marjie has several published studies that are available on Amazon: ***Choose Joy***, ***Live Happy, Just Jesus, I Believe in the Name of Jesus***, ***Be Brave I, Be Brave II***, and ***Your Story Matters***.

Marjie has been married to Steve for 31 years and together they have four children and one daughter-in-law. They live in the Seattle area.

Special thanks to these friends:

Love Squared Designs: made the beautiful bracelet shown on the cover and on the Chapter 2 title page. Here's how you can contact Lisa at Love Squared Designs:

Etsy: LoveSquaredDesigns.etsy.com
Instagram: @LoveSquaredDesigns
Facebook: lovesquareddesigns

2340 West Newton: made the beads shown on the Chapter 4 title page. Here's how you can contact Julie at 2340 West Newton:

Etsy: 2340WestNewton.etsy.com
Instagram: @JulieAnnePitta
thoughtsthatstick@blogspot.com

Kelly Johnson Art: painted the picture of the church shown on the Chapter 5 title page. Here's how you can contact Kelly at Kelly Johnson Art:

Facebook: Kelly Seresun Johnson
Instagram: KellyJohnsonArt@instagram
E-mail: Prjkdj@aol.com